Praise for *A Tune Both Familiar and Strange*

"These poems take us to places as far flung as Tasmania or Afghanistan, Israel or Iceland, letting us see across time and space into the lives of others, but also into the love and loss of Del Bourgo's own life. The strange becomes familiar as she braids her narratives with images so precise they seem cinematic. Whether elegies, love poems, or lyrics of wild imagining, these poems are marked by tenderness and compassion, even when the difficult or brutal is acknowledged. In the prose poem, 'A Gift,' we see 'overhead a hungry osprey on the wing. Wriggling in her talons, a fish. She will tear it to pieces for her nestlings.' This is a poet whose voice is sure and compelling and whose skills are as varied as the places she evokes so vividly."

—Lynne Knight, author of *The Language of Forgetting*

"Rafaella Del Bourgo's *A Tune Both Familiar and Strange* is the book of a lifetime, both in the sense that her first major publication is coming late in her life, and because it sweeps through that life, beginning with her Sephardic grandparents, their views and far flung travels, her own parents, her lovers, journeys, drug adventures, and much more, circling back to her beginnings in an afterlife. With moments of magical realism and comedy, she is movingly, quietly, startlingly insightful. Here, from early in the book, she writes of her father's hypocrisy: 'His kisses on my cheek/ bristle like points of a star.// See? Those are my tears/ dripping from his eyes.' *A Tune Both Familiar and Strange* is a debut not to be missed."

—Richard Silberg, author of *The Horses. New and Selected Poems*, Associate Editor of *Poetry Flash*

"Rafaella Del Bourgo has just gifted us with her new book, *A Tune Both Familiar and Strange*. 'My life,' she has written in one poem, 'has been composed of tessellated bits: meals, trips, jobs, books, men I have followed like a gypsy, or one of those wind-up toys that hits a wall and careens off in another direction.' Her poems are happy/sad, fearless/edgy, thoughtful/passionate, and about the clothed/unclothed as she propels us through Afghanistan, Iceland, Hungary, Portugal, Tasmania and countless other countries where her poems, set in these foreign places, are beautiful/wild/tender/serious/clever as she writes about Father, Mother, grandparents, strangers, lovers, animals, self. This book is amazing. You should read it!"

—Susan Terris, author of *Green Leaves, Unseeing.*

"Rafaella Del Bourgo's poems in *A Tune Both Familiar and Strange* are impassioned and attentive. She has a novelist's sense of narrative, an artist's eye for images, and a poet's ear for the music and magic of language. The poems are rich and varied, turning dreams and journeys into revelations and stories. Whether she is writing about her grandmother's life in Eritrea and Shanghai or cows at the kitchen window in Tasmania, you will want to hear what she has to say as you savor moments drizzled with sizzling olive oil and scented with lilacs. A fantastic book!"

—Lucille Lang Day, author of *Birds of San Pancho.* Co-editor of *Fire and Rain: Ecopoetry of California*

A Tune Both Familiar and Strange

Poems

Rafaella Del Bourgo

Regal House Publishing

Copyright © 2025 Rafaella Del Bourgo. All rights reserved.

Published by
Regal House Publishing, LLC
Raleigh, NC 27605
All rights reserved

ISBN -13 (paperback): 9781646036035
ISBN -13 (epub): 9781646036042
Library of Congress Control Number: 2024944561

Cover images and design by © C. B. Royal

The following is a work of fiction created by the author. All names, individuals, characters, places, items, brands, events, etc. were either the product of the author or were used fictitiously. Any name, place, event, person, brand, or item, current or past, is entirely coincidental.

All rights reserved. No part of this publication may be reproduced, stored in a retrieval system, or transmitted, in any form or by any means, electronic, mechanical, photocopying, recording, or otherwise, without the prior permission of Regal House Publishing.

All efforts were made to determine the copyright holders and obtain their permissions in any circumstance where copyrighted material was used. The publisher apologizes if any errors were made during this process, or if any omissions occurred. If noted, please contact the publisher and all efforts will be made to incorporate permissions in future editions.

Regal House Publishing supports rights of free expression and the value of copyright. The purpose of copyright is to encourage the creation of artistic works that enrich and define culture.

Printed in the United States of America

Regal House Publishing, LLC
https://regalhousepublishing.com

This book is dedicated:

To my father, Victor Del Bourgo, who never told me I couldn't do something because I was a girl.

To my mother, Dr. Sheila Helfman, who said, "I love you, honey, but poetry? I just don't get it."

To my brother, David Del Bourgo, poet and novelist, for his support and honest feedback.

To my husband, Carlos Runng, who, after a group poetry reading, always whispers to me, "You were the best one."

And to my poetry group, Lawrence DiCostanzo, Robert Coats, and Laura Schulkind for many years of friendly and constructive critique sessions.

CONTENTS

Foreword 1

So Very Hungry. 3

Kobe, Japan 5

Olive Oil. 6

Grandfather's Funeral, ...9

Sika Deer 11

Brass Key 12

Sunset. 14

Roses and Moons 15

Lost Art 17

Water and Salt. 19

Dear Father, ...21

Untended Saplings. 23

Swimming Lesson. 25

Streaky Dawn 26

Impact, 1955 28

Shut the Door 29

The Crying Room 31

Because. 33

On Spending Just One Night. 35

The Matah on Kibbutz Erez. 37

Drug Wars, 1971 39

Black Lizard. 42

In the Distance. 45

Two Jews, Truck Stop, Syrian Mountains 47

Afghanistan, Kandahar to Kabul, 1967 49

Dropping Acid in the Hindu Kush, 1967 51

Visions from the Khyber Pass, 1967. 54

Ship. 57

Iceland, Summer 59

At the Esztergom Basilica in Hungary. 61

Somebody Else's Life 63

   My Life as Jane Fonda 65

   The Baby. 67

   Hit and Run. 68

   Romany 69

   Winter, Lower Longley, Tasmania 72

   Imprint. 75

   Standing Dead. 77

A Tune Both Familiar and Strange 79

   Listening to Congolese Singer, Sam Mangwana 81

   Human Kindness 83

   Finally. 84

   Luna 87

   Dolphins in Shark Bay, Australia 88

   Cakes 89

   Underpants 90

   Improvisation in a High School Drama Class 92

   Masseuse 94

   I Keep an Apartment in Nome 96

   In a Berlin Bar 98

   Barking, Pt. Reyes. 100

Rooted in This Meadow 105

   Hank, Off-Leash, Pt. Reyes 107

   Exotic Feline Rescue Center 108

   The Road 110

   Noon. 112

   Sunday 113

Closer to the Ground 115

   Green River Cemetery 117

   Who We Are When They Are Gone 118

   November Song. 120

   Lilacs. 122

   Grief's Weird Sister. 124

A Gift 127
Into Night. 128
Bridge 131

Acknowledgements 132

FOREWORD

In *A Tune Both Familiar and Strange*, we encounter a life story in poetry—and what a full and rich—and busy—life it is, unfolding in these sixty poems, some going back more than one hundred years.

When so many poets of the moment seem to scream for attention, for likes and followers, Rafaella Del Bourgo, in a refreshingly direct and lucid free verse calmly recounts the crucial scenes and incidents that shaped the mature and grateful woman she is today.

The collection's opening section, "So Very Hungry," pays an appropriate first homage to parents and forebears, among them Sephardic Jews in the unexpected setting of Japan. Hers is a complicated legacy, as she recalls in "Grandfather's Funeral, Orthodox Sephardic Synagogue, Los Angeles," being excluded from the service along with the other females of the family, confined behind a screened-off balcony.

Her parents in particular are regarded without illusion: a loving father, who taught her many skills but could at times be undiscerning ("Swimming Lessons," "Streaky Dawn"), oblivious to his daughter's tears. Or a mother, challenging in her old age and decline, whom she memorably elegizes in a prose poem, "A Gift": "I wear her watch and feel her pulse beating in my wrist."

Recollections of youthful romances ("The Crying Room," "On Spending Just One Night With a Very Young Rabbinical Student") feature a narrator generally more experienced, or at least more assured, than her earnest boyfriends. And those poems give way to adventures in traveling, through the Mideast, Syria, Afghanistan, as a confident young woman in the tempestuous late 1960's. With titles like "Dropping Acid in the Hindu Kush, 1967," Del Bourgo captures the times, hitchhiking, reckoning with rifle-toting Bedouins on camels, even running with a dicey, vengeful crowd in Berkeley in "Drug Wars, 1971." More often than not, though, the speaker is surprised not by the hostility, but the hospitality, of the natives.

We are taken to all kinds of far-flung destinations in these pages—Iceland, Tasmania, Nome—and there are surreal touches ("Roses and Moons," "Black Lizard") and experiments in voice and persona, especially in the section, "Somebody Else's Life." Cats slip nimbly through these poems, and dogs romp on beaches at home in the poet's coastal California. The tone is serious, elegant, but not without humor, as in "My Life as Jane Fonda." If fated to spend adulthood as a celebrity lookalike, she certainly could have done worse.

Rooted as it is in autobiography, *A Tune Both Familiar and Strange* doesn't shy from the ultimate existential problems of faith and mortality. Consider the last stanza of "At the Esztergom Basilica in Hungary, the Jewish Atheist Lights a Candle for her Cat, Max" (the author has a penchant for the long title): "As for religious faith,/I leave that to those who provide/the candles./But still, I am drawn/to the ritual:/a spark to ignite the wick,/the radiance of the glow,/and, then all too soon,/the final melting of the wax,/the guttering of the flame"—how that suspended period leaves open (in direct counterpoint to the title) possibilities for belief and continuation, glowing with a radiance of their own.

And in "Winter, Lower Longley, Tasmania," when Rafaella Del Bourgo says, "I fear that the turn my life was supposed to take/has already happened," we are gratified by all the turns this life, and these poems, have taken. *A Tune Both Familiar and Strange* catches the ear "like music heard from far off," as Sherwood Anderson wrote in "Death in the Woods": "The notes had to be picked up slowly one at a time." How lucky we are to receive this harvest of a life lived through poetry.

—Peter Schmitt, author of *Goodbye, Apostrophe*
Final Judge, 2023 Terry J. Cox Poetry Award

SO VERY HUNGRY

KOBE, JAPAN

Under a sky the color of platinum and freshly cold,
the first home of my father's father,
I sit on the platform skirting a temple,
its yard, earth packed by a thousand years of feet.
On the margins, gravel and rock,
a monk drags bamboo tines
to create concentric circles
like ocean waves lapping against a boulder.

He glances my way,
a lone American woman
close to the cemetery where my ancestors rest.
He lays down the rake,
comes to sit beside me,
the map of his faith
in the folds of his shabby robe.

I show him a photograph from 1901,
my family,
Sephardic Jews against a painted backdrop,
obis tight around flowered kimonos.

He nods to a younger monk,
and his face blossoms into smile
as we are served bowls of sweet, hot tea.

Olive Oil

(for my Sephardic grandmother)

I remember eyes like sapphires,
dark moles in the folds of her neck,
her bosom, confined in linen.

Olive oil must be deep green and pungent
to evoke other memories:
sautéed fava beans, roasted chicken,
rice blushing with tomato and raisins plump with steam.
Cream puffs for dessert,
flour caught in her diamond ring.

We were fed advice:
 Never buy a used book; people are dirty.
 Those crab apples are sour;
 your mouth will pucker up and stay that way, forever.
 No one will want you.
 We don't take the bus; we'll never have to,
 God willing, we take cabs.
 Kosher meat is always best; don't try to fool me
 with that traife from Albertson's.
 If you touch the chow dog, wash your hands.

In her birthplace, Massua, Eritrea,
where she could hear lions cry outside the compound walls,
she attended the only school for girls;
nuns taught women's work.
On *Shabbos,* her father, a colonel in the Italian army,
brought in hungry Jews to feed.
Her mother emptied the larder, silently served them.

Before Grandmother's blood broke,
the betrothal was sealed by mail;
the family with its too many girls lacked dowry
and who but a cousin would have her?
Wrapped against the ocean's cold,
she was shipped to Shanghai,
hand-written recipes in her trunk.
Among the rickshaws on the dock,
an elegant stranger, in a downpour.

After twenty years and two boys,
before the Last Emperor fell, and before Mao marched,
Grandfather got the family and its fortune out,
settled into the house on Tiger Tail Road in Brentwood,
with its rose garden and view of the Los Angeles lights.

She ruled her house with a wave of her hand
and commands in Ladino.
She knitted and sewed,
taught the proper way to behave.
>   *Don't be familiar with the maid;*
>   *she's robbing us blind.*
>   *It's not ladylike to run.*
>   *Don't wear that frou-frou blouse;*
>   *dress well and you, too, can marry a Del Bourgo.*
>   *Keep the line pure.*

In her curio cabinet, animals of yellowed ivory, amber and jade:
a small herd of horses, three monkeys, a Pekinese.
Dressed up in dotted swiss,
I was allowed to play with them, but carefully,
behind the striped silk couch with dragon's feet.
>   *When I go, all these will be yours.*

But, after Grandfather died,
the antiques buyer with the mustache arrived.
Month by month, the creatures were sold
as I secretly wept in one room, Grandmother in another.

I wear her earrings of platinum and pearls,
make filling for *bourekas* the old way:
stir spinach and onions, ground meat
and garlic in sizzling olive oil.
I lean against the kitchen counter,
a knob of hard candy between my teeth,
sip bitter tea from her gold-rimmed cup,
listen for the sound of the lion's cry.

GRANDFATHER'S FUNERAL, ORTHODOX SEPHARDIC SYNAGOGUE, LOS ANGELES

We are separated in the foyer.
Father and my younger brother
invited into the great hall with the other men,
while Grandmother and I are barred entry.
Instead, we are ushered up interior stairs
to a gallery where women
and other teen-age girls
are concealed
behind a wooden screen.

We may not pray aloud nor sing.
We peer through leaf-pattern scroll-work,
our faces and bodies properly hidden,
as men raise their voices in praise of my grandfather.
The balcony is stuffy. It is hard to breathe.
The songs and prayers drone in my ears. Hebrew
by others for others.

My grandfather would drop a dollop of butter
into my soft-boiled eggs,
recite poems he'd written in Japanese,
and ask me questions each week
about how I was doing in school.
He never told me that a woman's role
was to be invisible,
her life's work, silence.

I long to fly down to the temple floor,
a raven with sharpened beak,
patrol back and forth
across the top of his coffin,
head raised toward heaven,
railing against the thief.

SIKA DEER

Winter. Kobe, Japan.
Among the upright stones with their vertical kanji,
lie the graves of my grandfather's people
under a lowering sky.

Their homes used bamboo for walls against
the white breath of winter, against
the music of the shamisen, three strings –
one for betrayal
by a business partner,
the second to mourn an infant
lost in this far-away land,
the last for the long letter from Turkey
that said: *Since the capstone has been removed,*
the archway to the family compound
is collapsing.

Beside my ancestors,
red maples reach up;
branches split against the gibbous moon.
Sika deer browse,
leave hoof prints in snow-light.

BRASS KEY

(IN 1956, NASSER EXPELLED THE JEWS FROM EGYPT.)

I peer at my grandmother's sister
in a family album.
It was long ago, the last time I saw her;
she is so like my grandmother,
the palest blue eyes,
the lips that smile and say,
Don't cross me.

She sits on the beach at Alexandria,
lacy sleeves, long skirt,
broad-brimmed hat
hiding her white, white skin
from the Egyptian sun.

In front of her, the grandsons,
born and raised there,
boys, red buckets full of sand,
building castles, stomping them down,
glancing up and laughing at the camera.

In the next photograph,
the whole family—my great-aunt,
her daughter and son-in-law, their two boys—
each with the one suitcase permitted,
stands on the ship's deck.
The father clasps a briefcase to his chest,
his left hand on his wife's shoulder.
She pulls her children close,
her head turned toward land,
as if torn between the blast of the ship's horn
and the clang of bells from a Coptic Church
on shore.

Listen to the salt cries of the gulls.
Smell the cold blue Mediterranean Sea.
Look at the two boys at the rail,
fat, creamy clouds above.
The boys are eating dates, spitting pits
at dolphins riding the bow wake.
Further along, in the shadow of the cabin,
see my great-aunt
clutching against her chest
the brass key to her home.
In her mouth, the metallic taste of exile.

SUNSET

Mother and I on grandmother's balcony,
Fuengirola, Spain.
We sip wine, break off chunks of still-warm bread,
eat brie with its thickened rind.

The Mediterranean just across the avenida.
Up the wide beach,
fishermen pull their small craft ashore,
bare feet sink deep into wet sand.

I love these birds.
Mother sighs. *I've been watching them every evening.*
She waves her hand at the sunset beginning to color clouds.
Black shapes dart against orange and gold.

These aren't birds, I inform her. *They're bats.*

She runs indoors with a shriek,
collapses onto the couch, shuddering.

What's wrong? I ask. *You loved them
two minutes ago.*

Mother glances at me, sniffs,
curls her feet up underneath her,
wraps an afghan 'round her shoulders.

She draws me close.
You don't understand, she murmurs
against the darkness.
*I loved them
when they were birds.*

Roses and Moons

Through the window,
a crescent moon caught
in the fingers of a quaking aspen.
The gold leaves remind me
of Mother's ormolu clock
with an inscription reading,
"Lost hours are never found again."

She lies in her bed, a great blue heron,
that patient hunter, atop her chest;
there is a blush of rose along its neck.
It is immobile for many minutes,
then plunges its dagger-sharp beak deep
into her breastbone.
She cries out once, twice,
then lapses into silence.

The bird cocks its head,
listens to the heart, still beating.
On a nearby table,
with a card from the sender, the requisite roses,
flower of love, stuck in a cut-glass vase,
the thick stems wrapped
with crimson ribbon.
The satin, pierced with thorns.

I am so very, very small
I live in her sweater drawer
among the cashmeres and merinos.
The drawer is always ajar so I can
stand on a rose-red cardigan,
peer over the edge.

If I were big enough, strong enough,
before it ever got near her,
I would chase away that blue-grey bird with a broom.
Let it perch on the horns of that moon
tangled in the aspen tree.

I would sit my mother up,
and feed her toast with marmalade.
As the clock eats time with its little wheels,
I would float the brush through her halo of hair,
then gently bathe her face, her shoulders and back
with the softest sponge,
and warm water scented with lavender.

LOST ART

I.
Pointillism.
Daubs of dove gray for her hair.
Deep-lake blue for the shadows beneath her eyes,
hollow of her cheeks,
and for the sweater I bring her to wear
over the hospital gown.
Her mouth breaks open as if to yawn in the new day,
but, no, she whispers and I lean down to hear.

I'd rather be at the shore, she says,
Large hat, picnic spread on the cloth,
crumbs of bread and bits of orange rind.
All the women, dots of color under shade trees.
The young men stand, dressed in black and white,
smoke cigarettes,
talk about their wives
as if they were children.
The sounds they make are solemn and dark.
This would be before their own babies were born.
Before the complications.

II.
Impressionism.
All the bouquets in thick, oily brush strokes,
swaths of melted color
make up for what's
missing from her skin.
Ranunculus-red, rose-bud pink.
Her bruised hands crossed upon the coverlet
as if she had already passed.

Vertical of a door, never locked,
curtain dividers not drawn,
horizontal gray for bed rails.
That wisteria wallpaper,
sweeps of lavender and purple, no barrier
to lives lived or left in nearby rooms.

I arch over her like a rainbow,
wipe her face with the satin binding of her blanket.

The nurse pulls aside heavy window curtains.
White floods every corner of the room.
I am blind.

WATER AND SALT

I.
His heart beat for sixty-seven years,
beat as he rubbed his cheek against my cheek,
stubble of beard, eyes closed,
the world briefly still.

II.
Father complains about the hospital food.
I rush to his house,
prepare gefilte fish his way,
three times through the grinder.
When I return, I find they had to jump-start his heart.

Back in his room
with the gefilte fish and some chicken broth,
I see how death takes a living thing apart.
At first, it is so mechanical.
The pump stops its labor.
Eyelids flutter closed, blood ceases circulation,
begins to pool.
Then the spectral palm reaches down,
scoops up that which is essential.
The bowl of broth starts to cool.

III.
As simple as water and salt.
Father raised me
to use hammer and drill;
to drive a truck and cook a meal,
spread butter on warm bread
after a noontime nap,
to eat the fruit and not the rind.

He told me this:
When it is unwise to sit down,
stand up.

I learned to repair a finch's wing,
to gentle a horse
with a hand upon its muzzle,
to glory in the friendship of a dog
who could race me as I ran,
who could teach me
to open my mouth and howl.

Dear Father,

This year I turn 67.
The age grandfather was when he died.
The age grandmother was when she died.
Your age when you died.

Since you left 30 years ago,
I have read 2,000 books—
if you count the mystery trash—
and loved every word.
I stopped eating the crusts of bread,
which always taste dry and burned,
even when they're not.
I balance my checkbook
like you taught me.

Husband number one
was a romantic error.
Father, I cut him loose and he flew free.
After several years,
I met husband number two;
29 years and counting.
He gently bites my shoulder
to wake me in the morning.

Look at the cat lifting her head,
love-eyes half-closed.
She's lying on our couch,
warmed by the sun.
And, look, on the sideboard,
there is one last piece of apple pie.

Father, I am still so very hungry.

UNTENDED SAPLINGS

SWIMMING LESSON

Hold your breath, hug your knees.
Father throws me into the deep end
of the pool.

I bounce on the bottom, then settle.
In my head, I sing a favorite song
while suns dance on the surface.
I am waiting to swim.

Then, air is gone and
bubbles no longer leak from my mouth.

Big splash, and a neighbor grabs my arm,
hauls me up and out of the water.

In my father's shadow, I shiver on a towel,
spit out chlorinated water.
I am five and refuse to let the others
see me cry.

She's so smart, my father blurts out.
I thought she would
just swim.
He shakes his head, brushes his hand
across his face, picks me up
so I can console him.

His kisses on my cheek
bristle like points of a star.

See? Those are my tears
dripping from his eyes.

STREAKY DAWN

In my childhood picture book
the father wakes up the little girl
into a streaky dawn,
layers of yellow and pink.
It's chilly.
She quickly dresses in her red and white pinafore
and her fingers fuss with the laces of her shoes.

The mother fixes them a hot breakfast;
pancakes swim in butter and syrup.
The girl even gets a rare mug of milky coffee
and she feels so grown-up.
Then, she and her father are off to the circus,
the pink and yellow dawn
now a clear blue sky.

When my father took me to the circus
I sat under the big tent and cried,
silently wiping tears on my sleeve when
he wasn't looking.
The elephants wore tutus while standing on tiny stools.
The lion tamer cracked his whip
as the lions and tigers
twisted their heads and snarled.
And little dogs in lime-colored vests
pranced on two legs while
sad monkeys with conical hats
pedaled tricycles.

This morning I opened the blinds,
looked out our bedroom windows,
saw the pink and yellow dawn
behind the coastal hills.
I thought of my father and how pleased
he was that day so many years ago
because we went to the circus together,
and how he told my mother
it was a such a happy time.

IMPACT, 1955
(FOR TR)

The meteorite rips through layers of roof,
through the ceiling
with sparkles embedded in the plaster,
and punches into her leg.

She has been clipping coupons,
watching *As the World Turns,*
and, yes, sipping some sherry,
then the world turned through its arc
just that fraction of an inch,
and boom,
she has a bruise
purpling her entire thigh.

The young boy sees these pictures
in *Life Magazine,*
the lady in her once-solid house
as she pulls up her yellow dress
for the camera,
turning away from her own nakedness,

and, in five minutes,
he tears the magazine into glorious confetti,
then gets on his bike
knowing now that it doesn't matter,
he can ride
anywhere.

SHUT THE DOOR

*

Father shuts the door when the baby is dropped—
thank god for the carpet. The children cry
though the baby does not and he feeds her
pudding from the tips of his fingers.

*

Close out the sound of his voice
teaching the children that cows say baa,
sheep lift their heads to bark,
and chickens growl, deep within their beaks.

*

In a long hall, Father holds Mother, sister holds baby,
bas-relief in green plastic chairs.
Brother sleeps in the hospital room, one kidney
resting in a dish, his eyes shut against brilliant pain.

*

At home Mother finds the note from that lady in the choir,
pink paper, sharp gilt edges.
It dares say, "Your wife is so lucky."
"Get the hell out of this house," Mother snaps at Father, "and
shut the door."

*

Close your eyes so we can't see Father in the rain
hauling boxes to the round, red car,
mother mopping the kitchen floor
like there was nothing in there he wanted anyway.

*

Now, where's Father? Sister's kissing that teenage boy,
his tongue a tourist in her mouth, hands traveling
her countryside. She laughs, pushes him up against the door.
Someone call an ambulance; she's twelve years old and on fire.

THE CRYING ROOM

On a fat summer day,
a month before school started again,
I walked out my front door
onto the cul de sac of Elon Avenue.
Alberto waited at the corner of Canterbury and Terra Bella,
safely away from neighbors' eyes.
He took my hand;
I could smell the spicy shaving cream
he didn't really need yet.
We walked the mile and a half
along Van Nuys Boulevard
to the Panorama Theater,
my saddle shoes slapping
hot pavement.

The theater's sign
reached into the sky.
For a double bill, fifty cents.
Popcorn and Coke, each a nickel.
He paid with money from his part-time job
at his father's corner store.
Through the left aisle's double doors,
a quick right turn took us
into a separate little room, soundproofed
for crying babies,
and nursing mothers.

But that day, we had the room to ourselves.
We settled in to velvety blue seats.
Put our food on the shelf.
I ate some popcorn;

my fingers got greasy.
We both faced the screen
through the large glass window.
The piped-in sound was a little tinny
as we watched Auntie Mame shock
her nephew. I sipped some Coke.

Alberto's arm snaked over the back of my seat.
He leaned over and gently kissed my buttery mouth
as his hand slid lower
to my already-full breasts.
What strange sweetness.
We closed our eyes.
Kissing became the main feature.
It became everything.

BECAUSE

Because his father was a haggard drunk,
roaring down their narrow street at night,
neck of a bottle clasped in his hands,
brick-dust caked under fingernails,
yelling his village tales.

Because his mother sat all day by the window,
bathrobe and scuffed slippers,
staring at squirrels,
four pots of coffee, two packs of Camels,
ignoring magazines from the old country.

Because my father wore a gray silk suit, blue tie,
briefcase bulging with client files and
his deft cartoons,
"Daddy at Work," a man like himself,
feet on desk, head lolling in sleep,
while the adding machine worked itself.

Because my mother was a psychologist,
patient with the melancholy, the mad,
who came home to a top drawer rattling
with the tranquilizer of the year.
In another drawer, candy bars
under panties and bras.

Because one August Tuesday
after high school graduation,
he drove me to the airport,
waited with me at the gate,
played his fingers down the flesh of my bare arm,
and said, "I'll always love you,"
as my flight was announced.

And because he'd already begun working with his dad,
making, he promised, very good money,
and that woman's voice demanding,
All passengers board now,
I backed him up against the observation glass
and kissed him one last time, so hard
it hurt us both.

ON SPENDING JUST ONE NIGHT WITH A VERY YOUNG RABBINICAL STUDENT

Night rain the color of shale.
I suggest something and he says,
Do people really do that? And I say,
I think they do.
Come with me. Let's try, if you dare.

And he does come,
but not too soon.

Fire in the bedroom.
Once, we break for sherry and chocolate.
Later, sheets in a turmoil, he says,
I could do this all night
and I say, *You're 18 and yes you can.*

Morning light.
Tender arrangement of limbs on bed
where, briefly, we are bound.
He says, *Maybe one more time*
then I've got to get back to school,
and I am underneath this landscape of muscle,
his skin smelling like fresh-baked bread.

Later, emerging from the bath,
he mentions the Hebrew word "chet,"
meaning not "sin" but rather "missing the mark,"
the archer having made a mistake
through lack of experience or skill.
I smile, towel him dry,
and he finds his clothes
underneath a chair.

After breakfast,
he leaves my house,
crunches away on the gravel path.
Underneath the yarmulke,
new strands of sunshine
woven into his hair.

THE MATAH ON KIBBUTZ EREZ

Three of us
in the non-citrus orchard,
work our worm-wires,
eighteen inches long,
finger loop at one end,
killing crook on the other,
inserting them into holes
in the slender tree trunks—
twist, pull, clean,
twist, pull, clean—
until the boss drives his tractor
south toward the Pardess, the citrus groves.

One more row for safety
then we fling our clothes to the ground,
stretching like wild cats.
Britte and Elke—
not sisters as many thought—
are pink and white
like the peaches
we were meant to protect.

I lie down in the hot dirt
as, holding hands,
they walk away
for a little privacy.

A tee shirt covers my eyes
but I can hear their distant laughter,
soft as the powdery dust between us,
can hear their small commotion of love
as worms lick at the heart
of the untended saplings.

DRUG WARS, 1971

It comes on.
I lie with Mike in front of the fire.
It surges through the bloodstream;
showers of sparks swim their way home.

Mike's friends at the table behind us
talk about killing someone. A rival dealer.

The television gets turned up.
Trying to cover their voices.
News announcer says,
Viet Nam. Body bags. Body
bags. Black plastic.

Lead him out into the blasted night,
along a tapering road, waning moon.
Shoot him down before he screams,
bury him fast.
Or, run him over; cover the body with a tarp
and let that be a warning.

I blink on with each breath in.
Off with each breath out.
The oak floor bites my bones,
pillow under my head stinks of long-ago dog.

Our hostess barks,
Those suggestions
just aren't practical.

A door opens and closes.
Someone enters. Someone leaves.
Clump of heavy boots,
muddy water sloshing in the corridor.

The monsoon. Two guys on guard duty;
one tries to light a joint,
muzzle flash,
the other is shouting and
something big explodes.

Arms and legs,
heavy and useless lengths of meat.

If I could move,
I'd drive out of Berkeley and never return,
clear across the country to Palm Beach, Florida.

Befriend an elderly woman.
Play Scrabble, stroke her cross-eyed cat,
walk home to a cottage
glistening in a sun-shower.
Fruiting banana trees, birds of paradise.

We swallowed gelcaps
in torrential rain.

Mike had said, *Pure pleasure.*
Pure pleasure
from the sassafras root.

The fire crackles, speaks
in a foreign tongue.

Right hand begins to burn,
to leak.
Drifts away from me.

Dust and grit,
a lost butterfly barrette,
one antenna cut off by a snake.
Slip it into a pocket
and now it's mine.

That woman at the table smiles,
offers us rum.
Don't tell
anyone, she hisses.
No. No.
My body is vibrating,
my jaw clamped shut.

BLACK LIZARD

I found a very small mummified lizard.
Black. Perfect toes, perfect tail.
Its eyes closed as if briefly asleep.
I lifted it carefully. Carried it home,
placed it on a scrap of white velvet
in a plastic case.
Put the case on my dresser top.

My lover said, *That is most unusual.*
I said, *I'll call him Lizlo.*

Events unfurled this way:
The lover was too young,
his knuckles unbloodied,
teeth white as the idea of youth itself,
and I sent him away to find.
He left behind only a shirt
printed with flowers, with sailboats.

     I've been to sea, I told Lizlo,
     when the waves folded like the pages of a book.
     At night in the harbor, the moon bled milk.
     I drank quickly so it wouldn't sour.
     At night in the harbor, the moon
     seeped a cloud of mist. I inhaled
     and filled my lungs with silver light.

In early morning,
I swam in circles with the fishes,
melancholy and noble.
Everything was splash.
Everything was chrysanthemum, delphinium.

Let me summarize matters for you so far:
I sent a young lover away to find;
I spent some days talking to a lizard,
perfect but dead.

This is what I explained to Lizlo:
I was grateful not to be a shark,
an eel, a jelly, a desolate narwhal.
I swam until I became blue,
and when I returned to the boat,
I no longer cast a shadow.

IN THE DISTANCE

Two Jews, Truck Stop, Syrian Mountains

Snow like powdered sugar on tree-tops,
on the twisting road.
Our truck driver brakes at a long mud hut. Beckons
to follow him inside.

Kerosene lanterns.
An older man and woman welcome him,
slant their eyes in our direction.
We are seated on cushions at a low table.
The three talk. Joe and I shiver with cold.

Other drivers arrive,
including one who looks like the actor Robert Mitchum.
He speaks a little English. Grins.
Your earrings are gold, yes?

We all sip tea.
The woman squats, cooks over a low stove,
little needles of heat,
the men in lively conversation.
Robert Mitchum steals a glance at us.
says, *You are going through Jordan to Israel, yes?*
His words, stones in the mouth.

Comfort food arrives at the table:
rice, flat bread, meat stew.
We do not ask what meat
but, somehow, it all smells like home.

I reach out with my left hand
and our driver slaps it.
Like an ignorant child,
I've done something wrong.
He fixes my plate the "proper" way,
shows me I should use my right hand.
More tea; the woman stokes the fire,
serves small pastries
stuffed with pistachios and honey.

Joe and I are ready to leave.
Robert Mitchum says, *We sleep.*
In a corner of the room,
the couple rolls out animal skins.

I lie down close against the wall, then Joe,
then our driver, Robert Mitchum,
the dozen other drivers.
More skins are laid on top of us.

We're no longer cold but Joe complains
the covers are too heavy.
Through the small window,
cedars burdened with snow
tremble in the wind.

I'm going to be raped,
I tell Joe.
I know, he says. *And I'll be murdered.*
Stabbed, probably, I say.
Yes, Joe agrees. *Stabbed.*

I start to laugh. Joe laughs.
Our truck driver and Robert Mitchum laugh.
It ripples down the communal bed,
all of us laughing and laughing.

AFGHANISTAN, KANDAHAR TO KABUL, 1967

Dawn. David and I hitch hike at the southeast corner of Kandahar, waiting for a ride with a crowd of laborers hoping to get home for their one day off. The sun rises, floods the valley. After two hours pass and a few oxcarts and boys on donkeys, the first vehicle arrives. A VW bus with a Dutchman, Bend Brouwer, and an English flower, Henrietta Blossom. We look to the laborers who had gotten there first. They wave at us to go. Maybe because of Bend's red mustache or Henrietta's porcelain skin. Maybe because strange goes with strange.

The interior of the bus, a fog of hash smoke, hazy and stuffy. Outside, sunny and still chilly, the high desert, encircled by white-capped peaks. We've barely begun when the front tire gets stuck in a pothole. Not on the road to Kabul. There is no road. We look at the vanishing tire, smoke more hash. North, closer to the mountains, a Bedouin encampment. David and Bend take off with their cameras, hope to snap some great shots by sneaking up on these fierce nomads who deal quite harshly with intruders. Henrietta and I sit on the hard-packed ground, lean against the bus. How silent the desert is, ocher and dun; blue mountains; clouds, wispy as an old man's beard.

In a funnel of dust, David and Bend run hard, pursued by five Bedouin fighters on camels. When our guys arrive, we lock ourselves inside the van, stash the cameras. But, it's too hot; we'd rather die with our feet on the ground. Line up to meet them as they rein in the camels. The men wear turbans, puffy shirts, puffy pants. Curly-toed shoes. At the waist, large, curved knives and, across the chest, rifles, ammunition belts. Their noses are long and narrow, skin the color of oiled walnut. Their eyes are cornflower-blue. The camels, decked out in woven red halters, tinkling bells attached.

We four stand at attention. Bend salutes. Breaks the silence; asks how to get to Kabul. The men don't respond, then the biggest one says, *Kabul,* points northeast, makes a motion indicating a distant pass like a long sleeve through the mountains. Bend nods to the five blue-eyed men, then asks, *Hashish?* The leader pulls a suede pouch from his waist, paper from a pocket. Forms a conical joint the size of a cigar; hands it to Bend.

Now we form a tableau: Bend, holding the joint; Henrietta Blossom blushing pink; David, hands behind his back; and I am thinking, *Aquiline noses? Blue eyes?* We are all still, even, for a moment, the camels. Only gathering cumulus, caught in rising air, cast shadows which drift across the scrub. The leader reaches toward his knife. Comes away with something in hand, leans down toward Bend. With a fleeting smile, he fires up a Zippo lighter.

Dropping Acid in the Hindu Kush, 1967

Early afternoon.
We eat milky Afghan caramels,
ignore the view below, the town, its river, the valley,
lie, instead, on our backs. Cobalt mountains,
the enormity overhead,
cloud parades:
columns of arabi sheep, camels with bright ornaments,
fanged and tawny cats.
A lone barbary falcon perched on a nearby outcropping,
its cry piercing and sharp.

Silent departure of the sun.
Confusion of night. We're hungry
and there is no map
for how to get back to our hotel in Kabul.
The path, narrow and rocky,
threads down into town,
through tiny villages,
clumps of mud homes, dimly lit,
a few laundry lines,
a communal well.

United in a chain,
we stumble past barking dogs
near where those German boys
had been stoned to death last year.
The barking becomes louder, closer.
Men emerge with lanterns, yelling.
We stop, breath held,
but they can see us and continue calling;

Come, come. We feed you supper.
Tomorrow, we reply.
Thank you so much,
tomorrow. Thank you.
Come, my wife make you supper.
That's what they yell at us, every one.

Back in town at our favorite restaurant,
western-style booths, cracked plastic,
and all the other customers local men.
Rice, lamb, and hot tea,
the radio crackling out Afghani songs,
one after another.

Barb and I exchange a glance,
amazed that we know this next tune from folk-dance class.
We stand up, join hands,
begin to tap-step in the aisles,
fast, complicated kicks and turns

we never mastered in college.
We are perfect. We are flawless,
two bodies in unison, the music
coloring the air, drifting up
to the hookah-stained ceiling.

When it's finished, we are still, panting.
Two young and careless American girls
eating in a neighborhood cafe
with our faces, our ankles showing.
Holding hands
and, in front of men,
forgetting ourselves in dance.
We do not know
that the Afghan culture is 3,000 years old,
but we do know all their women
are hidden away at home.

The men whisper among themselves
as if we could understand and be insulted
if they spoke out loud.
How much time passes? Many moments.
One man sighs, then claps. A second.
Some smile, their teeth brown, several missing.
Then, they all give in
and clap.

Visions from the Khyber Pass, 1967

Ribbon of road
1,000 foot drop
the bus careens around the curves
we are thrown
side to side in narrow wooden seats

Across the aisle
a young couple and their baby boy
his eyes crusted shut from some infection
I take out my Visine eye drops
put some in my eyes
again an hour later

I unwrap a pyramid of newspaper
pinch cooked rice with my fingers
pop it in my mouth
pale light
filters through dirty windows

The young father reaches his arm across
taps the back of my seat
holds up the baby
points to its eyes
then to my purse
with its little plastic bottle

I put a couple of drops
in each of the baby's eyes
gently wipe them
with a tissue
and the crust comes away

the boy coughs
opens his eyes
which are irritated and red
yet the mother's smile is hopeful

I fall asleep on my friend's shoulder
until the bus skids to a stop
we wonder if we've broken down
and who or what would ever come out here
to save us
the mountains jagged and brown
peaks dusted white
the sky dark gray and savage

The driver is talking to the man
in the seat behind him
who takes out his wallet to show
photos of his children
the photos are passed around the bus
as are more people's photos
and we are sitting mid-road
at the start of a vicious turn

The pictures include a hut
built against the side
of a mountain
two skinny dogs against
the blanket doorway
another a flock of shaggy goats
a teenager with a long stick

One man hears us speak English
and says a few words to us
I hand him the eye drops
say give this to the baby's parents
tell them to put in a drop morning and night

The baby's mother
hair covered in a black shawl
takes the magic bottle
the man translates
she says thank you nice American lady
may Allah bless you

Out the window now
flurries of snow
and a flock of magpies
flashing black and white
their calls briefly disturbing cold air

SHIP

Camel ride from the little beach resort,
south-east of Karachi.
She's feverish with malaria,
sailing through the desert in heavy seas.

Dunes and brush.
One might erupt into fire but there's no time to talk to God.
On her way back to town,
three story hotel, bed with sheets.
Doctor who speaks English and damn the money.

The others murmur,
part of the desert medley,
its gusts and bluster.
The camels grunt, air their complaints.
How the toes splay into the dirt with each step.
They are the way out and only way back.

She falls forward,
camel's golden hair clutched in her hands.
Her face against the rough blanket,
the smell sears her clothes, her skin.
Halter bells jingle a Bedouin tune
like lines wind-driven against a metal mast.

The tides—ships splash into water.
She says to the others, *Curse all mosquitoes,*
tries to smack the side of her neck.
She says to herself, *I must stay calm.*
Then, a fire storm;
someone's lit a match.

In the distance,
the horizon line wavers behind a stand of palms,
in front of them, a door, unhinged, half covered with sand;
words burned into the wood:
You thought you could trespass here.

ICELAND, SUMMER

Returning to the apartment I rented in Reykjavik,
I drive west past the fishing village of Hofn,
its channel to be navigated with care
due to the shifting patterns of the shoals.
The rocking boats, and the seafarers,
safe, for now, in the harbor.

To the edge of Jokulsarlon, the bay
where the glacier calves off into icebergs,
some small as travel trunks,
a few the size of a room.
Some are a celestial blue, some are banded
with dark streaks of volcanic dust.

The lagoon water licks at them;
the tidal pull draws them slowly
under the bridge
and, much diminished,
they sail off to be lost at sea.

Past the black sand beach at Dyrholaey
with its lava pillars rising up from the water,
and an arch stretching out past the waves,
which gives the area its name:
"the hill-island with the door-hole."

Two a.m. I return to my temporary home.
I push aside heavy drapes to see how
the "midnight sun"
paints snow-capped
mountains to the north
with a light, relentless and alien.

I collapse on the couch.
Crawling into my lap,
the resident cat I agreed
to care for during my visit.
He is heavy and orange,
like my tom back home,
brushes against my face, my hand.

I lean my head back.
I am a visitor here,
far from my home port.
This cat is my anchor.

At the Esztergom Basilica in Hungary, The Jewish Atheist Lights a Candle for her Cat, Max

I.
In the morning, Max would precede me downstairs,
ears flat back to reduce windage,
feet moving quickly in anticipation
of breakfast.
At the sound of the can opener,
he began to purr.
Later, he'd climb our 6-foot fence to survey
his domain.

Once, he ambled up
to a squirrel horizontal to the ground,
eating sunflower seeds.
He sniffed its behind
so delicately and with such respect,
the squirrel never stopped chewing.
Max cocked his head, went to lie down
beneath the lemon tree.

Before I left for Europe,
Max fell ill and died.
I missed his round body
asleep on my chest,
rising and falling,
rising and falling
with my breath.

II.
In Hungary, I climbed a hill to the 19th-century basilica,
built on the ruins of a much more ancient church.
I opened the heavy door to enter.
Inside, I lit a candle, and said his name, Max;
I plunked my coin into the little cup,
then sat in a pew and watched the reflected lights
dancing on the thick stone walls.

As for religious faith,
I leave that to those who provide
the candles.
But still, I am drawn
to the ritual:
a spark to ignite the wick,
the radiance of the glow,
and, then all too soon,
the final melting of the wax,
the guttering of the flame

AT THE ESZTERGOM BASILICA IN HUNGARY, THE JEWISH ATHEIST LIGHTS A CANDLE FOR HER CAT, MAX

I.

In the morning, Max would precede me downstairs,
ears flat back to reduce windage,
feet moving quickly in anticipation
of breakfast.
At the sound of the can opener,
he began to purr.
Later, he'd climb our 6-foot fence to survey
his domain.

Once, he ambled up
to a squirrel horizontal to the ground,
eating sunflower seeds.
He sniffed its behind
so delicately and with such respect,
the squirrel never stopped chewing.
Max cocked his head, went to lie down
beneath the lemon tree.

Before I left for Europe,
Max fell ill and died.
I missed his round body
asleep on my chest,
rising and falling,
rising and falling
with my breath.

II.
In Hungary, I climbed a hill to the 19th-century basilica,
built on the ruins of a much more ancient church.
I opened the heavy door to enter.
Inside, I lit a candle, and said his name, Max;
I plunked my coin into the little cup,
then sat in a pew and watched the reflected lights
dancing on the thick stone walls.

As for religious faith,
I leave that to those who provide
the candles.
But still, I am drawn
to the ritual:
a spark to ignite the wick,
the radiance of the glow,
and, then all too soon,
the final melting of the wax,
the guttering of the flame

SOMEBODY ELSE'S LIFE

My Life as Jane Fonda

In Costa Rica, lounging near the pool
of the Rose Garden Hotel,
I close my eyes, lay my book on my lap,
surrender myself,
as the sun makes false promises to my skin.
Ice cubes chill my lemonade
and the rippling of the water is soporific.
I'd like to take a nap, but suddenly my toe hurts.
I look up to see pruney eyes set in a biscuity face,
and a mouth that says *I know who you are.*
He is still pinching very hard
and I'd confess the truth to make him stop
but he doesn't want to hear, *I am not Jane Fonda.*

I've tried so many times; they just become ugly
at my arrogance and begin to yell
about who did I think I was,
movie tickets were not cheap,
and it does not pay to snub your fans.
One year earlier,
when on a first date with a very nice man
at a fine restaurant,
a lady tapped at my shoulder
and wanted my autograph for her daughter
who loved me in *9 to 5,*
I looked around at the tables of strangers
who cut their eyes at me.
And when I took pen in hand
and wrote *To Margie, a beautiful little person,*
Love, Jane Fonda,
tears welled up in this lady's eyes and she said,
You have made a little girl so very happy.

And now this man is still squeezing my toe
as if this were normal behavior.
He asks in a prim English accent
if I would sign the cafe menu.
I say *Yes, oh yes* and the pressure releases as I
scrawl her name.

He does not want to know that I live in an old Victorian house
stuffed with books and flocked with cat hair,
that I teach sleepy students by day
and read murder mysteries at night
in flannel pajamas fraying at the elbow.

He believes he is brushing up against the edge
of a satin and lace universe, and I have let him.

THE BABY

Even sitting here alone with him
it is hard to say out loud:
My baby is ugly.
His head, lumpy and flaking
red fingers
his kicking legs
and empty scrotum
trouble me.
I don't want to touch him
but his squalling irritates me so
I lift him gingerly
then hold him to my chest.

As I pace the small room
the heat of my skin
rapid beating of my heart
calm him
and he begins to gurgle
as if he were cute
and his life were going to be easy.
And he begins to smile
and that reminds me of his father.

Oh, that man was something
with his broad shoulders
and the dark, silky
swing of his hips.
He knew some woman would answer
every time he called.

HIT AND RUN
(FOR LS)

Teeth left scattered on the roadside verge,
my right eye gone,
face and body—
that of a patchwork woman
stitched together by a circle of aunties.

Scars journeyed through the color palette.
Bones knit, finally,
a white and silent craft.

After the driver's trial
my husband took me camping,
laid me on pine-needled ground,
made love to my Raggedy Ann body.

I felt our daughter catch inside me,
flung my hand above my head,
touched cool flesh of mushrooms
thrusting up
through the forest floor.

ROMANY

Traveling through Southern Portugal,
trying to escape the web of his celebrity.
He is still himself—
granny glasses, droopy mustache,
belly nicely furred and slightly convex so it
fits warmly into the curve at the base of my back
when I turn away from him in bed.

I'm still along for the ride.
He navigates narrow highways,
intent but relaxed,
because he can fix almost anything
with his Swiss army knife.
We've been together a very long time—
but don't call me his wife.

I admit, he tells me I'm beautiful,
and always laughs at my jokes.
Maybe that's enough.

In my lap, *People* magazine in Portuguese.
Clever Hollywood stars fluent in every tongue.
Chiclet teeth between crimson lips,
waterfall blondes. Those clothes
need no translation.

Orange groves and cork scrolling off oaks.
Me in a cowboy shirt and honky-tonk hair-do
tied up in a scarf,
feet up on the dashboard
painting my toenails "Damn-it-all Red."

On the right, rough laborers,
some, backs to the road,
pissing into the earth.
Last guy, built like wire wrapped around a tall spool,
is carving a wooden doll with a knife,
catches me watching,
flashes big grin.
From even just a glance,
I could see how exhaustion
has etched lines in his face.

We pass Romany gypsies leaning against old Lincolns.
They got everything right—
upswept pompadours, pointy patent leather shoes.
The women wear shifting skirts
as if the wind danced around them;
all the gold bracelets in the world
chime on their wrists as they wipe the dust off figs.

They seem happy doing nothing
for a while,
watching the cars go by.

Fado music on the radio,
those aching songs of unrealized dreams.
I'm singing full voice,
making up my own words,
about gypsy caravans
and men at the side of the road.

My lover says
he always did like figs.

Sometimes I think he is eating
the sweetest years of my life.

Sometimes I eat his fame.
Sometimes, but not always,
it isn't enough,
and I feel like I'm starving.

WINTER, LOWER LONGLEY, TASMANIA

with a butter knife I scrape
frost off the inside of the kitchen windows
and there they are again
cow faces with their dark eyes
noses breathing steam
feet stamping in the snow

like the lamb
from the farm up the hill
and the black cat
they want to come in
they want to come in out of the cold
into the house which will be warm
as soon as the logs catch

on the table six ripe apricots
blushed with sun
plump with sweet water all the way from California
flown in then purchased at great expense
from the one market in town

I open the door for the cat
then shut it quickly
against the lamb and a possible cow stampede
sip a cup of coffee
with milk and sugar the way I like it

as snow continues to drift down
the cows wear white caps
white as the lamb who has kicked down his fence again
and is huddled on my back porch

two possums snuffle
snouts to the ground near the woodshed
looking for something to eat
from the Marsupials of Tasmania poster
I learn they are brushtails

Sulphur crested cockatoos winging overhead
screech like rusty hinges
the cows moo in response
the cat wakes up raises her head and yawns
these sounds and the occasional
brush of a lone car on our country road
are all that interrupt the silence of falling snow

we have no radio and no phone
we brought ten albums with us
and I've listened to them so often
that now I'm yelling at Waylon Jennings
Either go to the rodeo with Willy
or grow up and stay with your pregnant girlfriend
but whatever the hell you do
just stop your damn whining

I slept all night yet I'm so tired
my husband
is dazzling them at the university
and I fear that the turn my life was supposed to take
has already happened

I am sitting here alone
cows smearing my windows
with their noses and tongues
tilting their heads right and left
the cat on my lap
the lamb taken from the flock
as a plaything for the farmer's sons
still desolate on my porch

I'm watching the fire burn
and waiting to warm up
and maybe just maybe this is it
even though I'm living somebody else's life
maybe this is the turn

IMPRINT

Just as I will love your handwriting forever,
even after your betrayal,
when nothing in your pockets could buy back the past,
so too, pieces of my life
continue to bear your imprint.

Here in my jewelry box, the scarab ring from Melbourne.
On the floor, a kilim rug we bought in Turkey
from the mustachioed man who insisted we marry.
And, in the kitchen, ceramic plates you made when I complained
that I lived with a potter
but ate off dishes from the Goodwill.

The ring could be sold and the money squandered,
the rug rolled up and stuffed in a dumpster,
the plates smashed one at a time
against a crumbling brick wall,

but, one street in the heart of town
must be crossed and re-crossed.
There's the cottage you lived in
with your sweet-tempered setter
languid on the couch.
Pairs of cowboy boots lined up in the closet.
Triumph motorcycle
used as a plant stand.

I remember:
Mt. Rainier in May, clear sky.
You have thrown down a green-suede cape.
We are naked in the center of the world,
scribble our love on the mountainside.
Your arms are warm.
The sun is hot.
And my hands and feet
burn in the snow.

Standing Dead

You hear them say his name
as if it still belonged to you
though the syllables had not made sense
of your world
for more than a year.

He took, of course, everything:
the old Packard
parked behind a line of oaks
and the young hound,
a gold watch
grandfather had bequeathed you,
four hundred dollars
hidden under lingerie,
the hazel color from your eyes.

You rummage in a dresser
to find what he left:
one picture of a giraffe,
drawn as a gift,
its mouth closed,
eyes hooded,
head turned to the side.

You wonder what these others know
of this invisible blight,
of leaves that slowly discolor
and begin to die,
leaving a remnant,
a trunk, some branches.
You press fingertips to your wrist
and are surprised to feel
the sap still running.

A Tune Both Familiar
and Strange

LISTENING TO CONGOLESE SINGER, SAM MANGWANA

Open doorway.
A cot inside the steamy darkness,
the child dangles skinny legs,
smiles with all of his seven years.
His mother counts coins,
drops them into her special box
and another dress is done now,
the seams straight,
the hem even.
He feels the cotton, sucks his thumb.

Drums across the courtyard. The men drink beer.
Sam Mangwana's band sings *Balobi*;
barefoot dancers kick dust,
step lightly on each other's toes.
Sam is hoarse;
his face glows in red light.
On the margins now, the boy
shapes the words with his mouth.
His mother tugs his soft, thick hair.
You think you know this life?

Bright words spill out
of Sam's purple lips.
The boy pokes his finger in the gap
between his teeth;
with the other hand
he holds his pet chicken,
its head tucked into his armpit.
Before dawn, the boy wakes up hungry.
The moon, a hammered silver platter,
mothers hand-stitching by its light.

HUMAN KINDNESS

At the base of the off ramp
he sat on a plastic crate,
slouched, his sweatshirt hood
almost covering his eyes.
The sign on the ground,
attached to a basket,
said, "I'm grateful for any little
human kindness."

Waiting at a red light,
I fished in my purse,
grabbed a dollar,
lowered the window
and called out to him.
He slowly rose,
his young, weathered face
smiling a bit
as he took the money.

Then, much more animated,
he cried, *A bee* !
What? I asked.
He repeated, *A bee.*
You might get stung.
The light turned green but
the cars behind me did not honk
as the young man stuck his head and arm
through the window,
found the bee,
gently guided it outside,
and then returned to the shadow
of the overpass.

FINALLY

You are the struck match,
the incandescent father,
the great physician
who cures the babies and the princes of the world,
who receives a thank you gift from Egypt,
a Mercedes Benz the color of a pearl.

When you leave for work
Mother rises from the table,
takes her special cup from behind the sugar bin.
I see how she measures
and measures again
and how she sips the liquor into herself.
It warms her and she closes her eyes.
Later, I watch as Mother eats veal with her friends
and says, *Yes, of course, he's terribly busy.*

Last month
in a magic moment,
you rested the weight of your steady hand
upon my head
and I began a sweet dissolve
until I heard you say *She is too thin.*
Shut up in my room
I threw your photo to the floor
then lifted it up again
to rest in the top drawer
between socks stretched out at the ankle
and a black silk camisole
you won't ever let me wear.

It is always dark and cold
when you finally come home.
We are carved into our designated chairs.
You tell us about the hospital.
We wait for you to begin
before we eat.
You ask me those questions
about how I am doing in school
and, like a lady,
I must set down my fork.
If I answer correctly
you smile, and I may resume my meal,
but if I do not, you frown
and I must continue until you smile
and then I may eat again.

It is nine o'clock, time to be fed.
Mother passes the roast,
hoping I will reach for her food,
but I am not hungry.
And, no, Father,
since you asked,
there is nothing I have done,
nothing of consequence.
You have saved the world;
I have just breathed air,
taken a sip of water,
eaten one crust of bread.

IDA'S WINE

Aunt Ida lies in a pale violet dress.
It suits her, my cousin tells me.
It does, regal like the sky toward the end of dusk
when starlings line up on wires over dogwood trees.

The cemetery, autumn drizzle.
Above the solemn mourning clothes,
a disorder of umbrellas the colors of a circus.
She is lowered into her final bed
and I steal away from the grave.

Back at the funeral parlor
the undertaker, my ex-husband,
leans over an open casket,
touches up someone's eyebrows with a pencil,
velvety and black.
He straightens, sucks on a forbidden cigarette,
sips a Coke and his whole body moans with pleasure.

When I call his name,
he croons, *Ah,*
my beautiful first wife,
and, even among those coffins,
even beside the newly-dead,
even though we have just buried my favorite aunt, Ida,
the compliment burns my cheeks.

He's forty now. Heavier, but looks fine.
Open-heart surgery scar hidden under the sharp white shirt.
Married to that girl with a simple name.
She works at the nail place;
stabbed me once with cuticle scissors.

I kiss him on the mouth
and taste the sweet sizzle.
Walk the tightrope to my cousins' house,
eat cake, get a little drunk on
Ida's elderberry wine.

Luna

I slide into bed, pull the chenille
over my head and dream of a painted trio
like Chagall's lovers drifting around the moon,
brushed by, charmed by,
an angel, milky white and naked
in the hours of royal blue.

I pucker up in the dark,
kiss the night,
and am hurled
outside of the house where bees
have died brittle on the windowsill,
given up their buzz and fizz,
trying so hard
to get out through the panes of glass.

I am hurled up and through the night,
out of earth orbit,
toward Luna which waxes and wanes.
Now there are no windows or walls,
no fuzzy carcasses yellow and black.

Here there are just
those lovers,
that winged angel,
the alabaster moon,
a small and grinning goat,
and me,
floating, floating.

DOLPHINS IN SHARK BAY, AUSTRALIA

In lazy circles they cruise the shallows,
heads up, hungry for the air,
and, maybe, for the sight of land.

One slides along my legs and
when I reach down to stroke her rubbery skin,
she smacks her tail like a cranky aunt
tired of company already.

A nudge behind my knees
and here is another with a fish in his mouth.
I take it gingerly, avoiding his white picket teeth
and, glad the fish is dead,
caress the animal's warm flank,
read the billboard near the high-tide mark:
If a dolphin gives you a fish. Keep it. Returning a fish
is bad manners.

One dolphin swims to a yellow lab
standing up to his chest
in cool blue ocean.
The dolphin pushes her beak into the dog's black nose,
rubs her face against coarse fur.
A woman on shore calls, "Magic, Magic,"
but the dog does not move.

The dolphins gather
wearing their grins,
then swim west and disappear from sight.
The dog and I stare after them,
the fish, a cold and slippery weight
in my hand.

CAKES

Don't bother, she told me.
Nothing you say will make me feel guilty.
She sat in the kitchen after removing all the frosting
from one of my freshly-baked cakes with her index finger,
a circle of chocolate around her lips,
while other guests talked in the living room.
There were no words in my mouth.

The scene was bathed in light
as I whipped cream and sliced strawberries.
The frosting was our secret, Rosemary's and mine,
and, years later, she painted us onto a canvas:
Rocking chairs on a wooden porch
in a silent neighborhood.

One, honeyed hair a confection, piled up
and held fast with tortoiseshell pins,
nibbles a slice of almond torte.
The other, her head covered with ravens' feathers,
legs crossed under a red satin skirt,
reaches toward a nearby table
for a piece of gingerbread.

Cirrus clouds are brushed
against the California sky,
and the sun yellows everything,
the bulbous 1942 Dodge waiting at the stop sign,
and the cars parked in a string at the curb.
Citrus trees line the roadway.
Two women, Sunday afternoon.

Underpants

Summer 1966, downtown L.A—bums and business people. My boyfriend drops me off two blocks from Sears Roebuck, west coast headquarters. I am 21, the assistant buyer for ladies' lingerie and lounge wear for all stores west of the center line of the United States. My boss, the head buyer, is never there. Saul is bald and strangely sexy, lunches with his Greek wife who doesn't like to eat alone. "Don't worry," he tells me early on. "There's not that much to do."

They call my secretary the Roadrunner; she speeds down hallways with a fervor. I sit at Saul's desk, press the intercom and she's there with steno pad. "Coral," I say, "take a letter." She licks the tip of her pencil, straightens the tweed skirt, pats tight curls.

"Dear Mr. Stevenson." "But he's the company president," she says. "Dear Mr. Stevenson," I continue. "It has come to my attention that this jewel of a secretary, Miss Coral Black, has been mistreated by this organization in that etcetera etcetera." "Oh." She blanches. "You mustn't say that." "Because of her long service to this company and the fact that her name is composed of the two most popular colors for underpants this season, Miss Black deserves to be treated with the utmost respect."

"That makes no sense," Coral Black tells me, covers her mouth to laugh. "Furthermore, both Miss Black and myself have been daily denied the candy rationed out to all other employees." "The secretaries actually buy it themselves," she reminds me. "And this situation, both criminal and uncivil, must be immediately rectified. We will accept the following: Hershey's Kisses, Marshmallow Peanuts, Moon Pies."

"I love them all," Coral says. "Butter mints, caramels, and anything made by See's in milk chocolate would be most acceptable. We need our fuel." "The others make fun of me because I fly down the halls," she says. "Slowing down would take so long. I'm 42 and live with my mother—I'm always in a hurry."

"Mr. Stevenson, if substantive changes are not implemented immediately, Miss Black and I, in concert with our attorneys, will be forced to etcetera, etcetera, and severe consequences will surely follow. Imagine this corporate headquarters in chaos. Or in flames."

"Ah, the fires of hell," she says. "I write hymns in my spare time. Do you go to church?" "No," I say, "I'm an atheist." "For always?" she asks. "Yes, for always. I came out of the egg that way." "Oh!" she says, and then, "I've never met an atheist before. I thought they might be...taller."

"My boyfriend is one and IS taller. Black," I say. "Drops me off far from here because of the etcetera, etcetera."

"Yes," Coral says, "I know. The shock in the store below, the dark arm and the white arm, brushing. That woman was very upset. The world of fashion can be so cruel."

IMPROVISATION IN A HIGH SCHOOL DRAMA CLASS FOR TROUBLED TEENS

You are dogs waiting to see the vet,
I tell the two girls best known
for their skimpy skirts and combat boots
and for the many days they take the bus to the beach
to hustle military guys.

The girls squat on chairs
their hands drooping under their chins
to represent paws.

Are you scared? The first dog asks
and the other growls
then lunges as if to nip.
I'm always scared here, she says.
They hurt me.

The yellow-haired vet isn't so bad
the second dog says at last.
Gave me dried liver after a shot.
The yellow-haired vet, the first dog says,
hurt me when I was just a puppy.
The other draws back her lips
reaches around to chew at fleas
on her flank.

Well, is your master nice? the first dog asks
and the other shakes her floppy ears.
He tells me to do things and when I'm slow
he yells.
I had a nicer one before

but he wrapped me in a towel
and gave me away.
She scratches her neck.

My master gives commands,
the first dog says,
and if I don't understand
he slaps me on the snout with a slipper.
Her wet, black nose twitches.
Oh, they just called my name, she says.
Throws back her head
and begins to yowl.

Masseuse

he was naked
on his stomach
her hands were on him
and had been on him

and because he was short, soft and overweight
she probably wouldn't
understand how strong he was
how strong he could be

her hands
cinnamon-scented oil
and in this over-heated room
music from someplace with
astonishing mountains
where hearts are forced
to beat too fast

and incense
a hot breeze lifting lace curtains
the muscles of his back and legs
coiled and tight

and because she might not know
that a plain-looking man
could be a fine lover
could make a woman like her shiver

with both arms
he reached under that flowing dress
for the twin globes of her ass
and he waited for her to sigh
and kiss his neck

and when she slammed him
on the side of his head
with her fist
he quickly felt like a wind sock after a storm
and his ears began to ring
like the Tibetan bells chiming
in the background
to enhance personal enlightenment
and well-being

I Keep an Apartment in Nome
(for MM)

Why shouldn't I escape to the Arctic Circle? The voices in my head grow quieter here. Who says we must suffer the cacophony, the unbearable sulphur-yellow sun, clogged arteries of southern California?

Pacific Coast Highway. Tourists fat like ticks. Girls, string bikinis and devil tattoos. Who says we must suffer mishandling by the police, shoved against a wall, the burr of brick against cheek? Stab wound in my palm, yet I'm hauled off for psychiatric evaluation.

Winter. Handcuff cold. I have my fevered friend, the stove; I knit sweaters, dove grey, seventeen so far and no one to give them to. In California, doves feed on my porch.

Three windows—a triptych on the Bering Sea. By day, I watch the sun try to rise against the frigid pewter sky. Storms roll in. Bloody clouds. At night, the aurora borealis, purple and green.

I eat chocolate, bittersweet under the moon. On the floor, polar bear rug, wine corks on claws. Mother said, *Glass eyes see no evil and only the filbert tree is nuts.* I can still hear her.

March. End of the Iditarod. Spectators watch dogsleds cross the finish line. The sky splinters; hungry wind bites my lips, my chin. I become lace; snow blows through me.

The dogs wear leather booties. Rime tips their fur. The winner kisses his dogs' snouts, their ears. A dozen ecstatic dogs. A dozen ecstatic kisses.

Sundays, church. I go, too. Cross myself, press my fingers to my mouth. Candle flames. The Lamb of God. Lamb of God. Clementine, the caribou, velvety brown, folded onto the snow. How quiet she is, and wise. She, too, has survived winter's hard, hard love.

In June, birders arrive. Widows from Waukegan. Insurance brokers from Burlingame. Thank goodness my policies are current. A young girl with deep scratches. I hand her Band-Aids. *Oh,* her mother says. *You must be a nurse or a mommy.* No. I am a woman who tears at her cuticles until they bleed. I am a woman who harms herself.

Yellow ptarmigan. Aleutian terns. Jiggy with excitement, we raise our glasses. Someone mentions Newport Beach, my other home. I set my jaw so I won't cry out.

Unraveling, I sit near three ladies at lunch. Slaty-backed gulls and bacon sandwiches. The ladies talk about the rivers and wetlands, the high alpine tundra. Does landscape shape a life?

Here, all summer, day and night are fair. I keep time by the water clock, the tide clock. Minutes and hours, days, move in and out over the shoreline like crabs. At night, I dream of forests where a person could hide. Wake up disoriented, jaggy.

Summer's last birding tour. Fall migration. Red-throated loons, sand hill cranes. At the visitor center, we record the birds we've seen. One man near me says, *Crazy as a loon.* I say, *Ha ha ha. And, yet, I'm here.*

In a Berlin Bar

Stella says it first,
I am not a lesbian.
I say, *I'm not one either.*
On the stage, a full orchestra,
warm thirties jazz.
Men, mostly dressed in glittery hats and straps,
dance with other men,
and the women in three-piece suits,
striped, and ties,
dance with other women.

The slender man I came with,
who is not enough of a woman
or is too much of a woman,
is dancing with Stella's pretty brother
who is wrapped in a red silk dress.

Outside, winter snow.
Inside, my friend laughing,
head tipped back, his white throat exposed.
Stella glances at him.
Says, *I have faith. God*
does not pay attention to what we wear.
God does not make judgments about who we love.
I've heard this before and shrug.

She is plain. Chalky moon-faced,
flat eyes the color of slate.
She is also in a silky dress,
keeping time with her lacquered fingernails
on the table top.

Come on, she tells me. *We might as well.*
I'll be the girl first,
then we can change.

We make our way onto the floor.
She places my right hand on her waist,
which is both tender and firm.
Rests her left hand on my shoulder.
Stella's good; we move easily to the music,
a tune both familiar and strange.

BARKING, PT. REYES

in the dark gloss of night
he is barking and I am awake
he's barking at raccoons fighting to get into
his food on the front porch
at the orchard
where a flock of quail with sequins for eyes
hunker down for cover in a nest of wild grasses
and deer will eat pears at dawn

barking at coyotes
yipping on the wetlands of Tomales Bay
great blue heron taking flight into splintered cold
three in the morning
he is barking
at the strange man
creeping around
with the long sharp knife
trying to be quiet on the gravel driveway

at termites chewing up the foundations of the house
at the war Far Away
financial meltdown
at glaciers melting in Greenland and at the poles
crash and splash
somebody's child patient at the bottom of a pool
barking at a flock of wild turkeys
one male gobbling from his roost

he is barking at a car veering off the road
at ravens glossy and moonless
like the night of my senior prom
sapphire blue strapless dress
white gardenias at the waist
with the guy who asked me
not the guy I wanted to ask

barking
the complexity of health care
frightened citizens sequestered in their homes
bodies piled up in refrigerated trucks
and another friend has died
one more name to cross out
of my address book

or because the whole East Coast was shivering with cold
the West Coast red-hot on fire
smoke turning blue skies to dark red
sweat dripping down the back
hurricanes washing away the southern Coast
barking because poisonous squid
hide deep in cracks between rocks
or because there are no poisonous squid
off the coast of California
just millions of sea urchins devouring the kelp beds

barking at sleeping quail
bobbing head-feathers
on a moonless
three in the morning
he is barking
at coyotes chewing off the edges of Tomales Bay
100 yards west of us
San Andreas Fault
silently tearing the whole earth apart

barking my thumb has started to hurt
I can't open jars
my friends have lines in their hair
their faces are worried and grey
the dark gloss of night
owl nesting in the cypress
the long sharp creeper
he is barking at the knife

venomous young men barking mad
want to shoot, want to explode
and marchers in the streets
wipe tear gas from their eyes and weep
barking because there are no poisonous squid
just black ink as they vanish
black ooze of oil in the Gulf of Mexico
brown pelican on a nest of poisoned eggs

because of the soldiers dead and alive
lost in the mountains
of Far Away
the rattle of the metal can
raccoons on the front no
because of the earthquake
another country Far Away
buildings broken into fragments
the mothers who grabbed their children too hard
made them cry the mothers who couldn't rescue

he is barking at the folding of cloud upon cloud
rosy shawl around the shoulders of the moon
in the earliest part of morning
the dark gloss still on the night
quail black sequins for eyes
hidden among cattails near the pond

late rain storm on the horizon
at the noise like a car door slamming
the strange knife
termites demolishing the foundation of this house

men and women snow-tipped mountains
or thirsty deserts of Far Away
he is barking at Bedouin camels, no
at miners deep underground
singing their national anthem
with coal dust in their lungs
he's barking for the capsule to ascend from the bowels of hell
and all those still buried under rubble Near and Far Away
the owl shudders in the cypress

barking at the still no jobs empty wallet
people with sequins for eyes
waiting in line for water and food
waiting in line for medicine and pears

now he is asleep dreaming of his walk on Limantour Beach
people stroking his head big black dog beautiful dog
the strained light wet on pink sand

I am at the window
because of the orchard
where deer eat succulent
in the long sharp in the moonless
raccoons chase one another
chittering among the trees apples and pears
Far Away and very close

I lie down beside him on the dog bed
my face my hands in the fur of his neck
I kiss his velvety ear
his breath slow now and rhythmic
his feet remembering the pink wet sand

somewhere in the still dark
someone is whistling
people and animals cross over a bridge
while out by the pond the quail sequins for eyes
and overhead the raven
flies invisible

ROOTED IN THIS MEADOW

Hank, Off-Leash, Pt. Reyes

We're at the end of the walk where
the trail splits;
left returns to the parking lot,
right slopes down to Tomales Bay.
Hank, off leash, looks over his shoulder at me
and I say, *No.*
We're not going to the beach today.

It is an April morning at the close
of my seventh decade.
The hills across the road are green from spring rains
with brushstrokes of orange poppies and purple lupine.
Overhead, a small celebration of clouds
against an azure sky,
and I feel the sting of sun
on my bare arms and the backs of my hands.

Hank feigns disinterest,
then, ears flapping,
bolts for the beach, the salty water
and a long, forbidden swim. I follow,
sit on a log to wait for him
as ripples fan out along the shore.
I sift through the sea-smoothed bits of glass,
the small stones at my feet,

find a reddish heart, and one the color of jade
which I pocket for my collection.
Hank's tail wags as he bounds my way,
rolls in the sand,
then knocks against my legs, presses
his cold nose into my face.
He is so very, very happy.

Exotic Feline Rescue Center

Stay behind the red line, our guide says.
The panther turns with a growl. One great leap
and she hurls herself against the cage, then hunkers
down on her haunches; yellow eyes follow his approach.

When he's within arm's reach
she opens her jaws, full set of predator's teeth
guarding the rose-pink tongue. He slips his fingers
through the chain-link. She closes around them
and begins to suck, as if his hand were coated
with blood, a panther's version of honey. Her eyes
shut, muscles still and quiet.

He's worked here six years, ever since he retired to this
little town from the clamor of L.A.
He'd been an airline pilot, decorated captain.
He missed the hailstorms and fog-bound landings,
that sense of himself filling the cockpit.

His wife has her doubts,
tells him he's a fool to waste his time
with stinking beasts who mauled a volunteer
just last spring;
how bored he'd gotten watching game shows on TV
and pretending he liked to garden.

He explains the history
of their mountain lions, snow leopards, lynx
and margay. Dips his chin, says, *These are not just
mindless creatures, not just organic machines.*
I say, *Beautiful, this cat.*
He says, *Sweet, too. My girl.*

She's drooling, black fur waffled against the wire,
breathing slowed as if she were in another world
He glances at his watch, puts his finger to his lips, whispers,
*The most dangerous thing I do these days
is trying to get my hand out of the panther's mouth.*

THE ROAD
(FOR MM)

Just for a moment
    I lost
        myself.
When I woke, the Jeep and I were
    upside down.
I released the seat belt, crawled out
        the window.
We were in a meadow.
It might have been
    spring.
The field was dappled
with color.
        Purple and yellow lupine,
        buttercups,
    white iris with their ruffled
    dragon faces.
Nearby, a herd of deer.
Several does, fawns and a buck
who lowered his head and pawed the ground.
    The others were   behind him,
    eating flowers and grass.
    The blossoms decorated
    their mouths.
The buck drew closer, snorting.
    I told him I was   hurt
    and he became quiet.
My legs ached and my arms.
Blood on my head.
I could feel it warm and red on
my fingers.

Blood on my pale blue blouse.
                    The sound of hooves, swishing
            through grass and the slight
                    slithering
                    of a pale green snake.
A country road at dusk.
Grass and flowers and deer and one skinny
little snake,
        an upside down   yellow box of a car,
        a woman, listening
                as a siren
                    drilled   the sky.
The deer moved
                away from
                    the road.
I waited   on my back
                    and watched the sun   slide down
                                behind a hill.

Noon
(FOR MY HUSBAND)

His dirty, raspberry-colored hat,
tipped back.
He rests below the lemon tree,
fragrant stars and sour suns,
left arm under his head,
his thumb-nail black
from a hammer stroke.

Wedding ring, its scratches and nicks.
Coveralls speckled with dust and
torn at the knee.
The gold bracelet
—heavier twin of mine—
slides as he rubs the cat's generous belly;

she stretches and shuts her eyes.
Beneath the glossy green canopy,
his eyes close, too—
like a young boy, late June,
re-learning the language of summer.

Sunday

I am rooted in this meadow.

Under my feet,
below the forest of grass blades,
mouse has lined a burrow with bitter herbs,
sleeps comforted
by the weight of darkness.

Iridescent beetles next to the pathway
dig parallel tunnels into horse dung;
around my head,
pairs of dragonflies
rhyme couplets on the wind.

Swallows fly so high
in the blindness of this day,
they weave in and out
of the constellations
I cannot see.

CLOSER TO THE GROUND

GREEN RIVER CEMETERY

From across Accabonac Road, I look out
at those who have stumbled and fallen
into the arms of the earth.
The country of the interrupted.

Sometimes, rain that might have drowned them.
Sometimes, drifts of snow
on the ornamental boulders,
on the standing grave stones.

It is April.
An old neighbor has died.
Last night, before the funeral,
her daughter placed four dozen
long-stemmed white roses
around the grave site.

This early morning,
sun streams through the window.
I open it.
The air is still and quite cold.
In the wet grass, I can see
footprints of deer,
and four dozen stems with thorns.

WHO WE ARE WHEN THEY ARE GONE

My parents
have taken up residence in my body,
like ex-pats who have abandoned their homes
and chosen to live in a foreign place.

Sometimes my mother's voice
bursts forth from my lips
saying things to a child, like,
We do not spit at people.
We do not ever spit.

And my father, inside my head
with his jokes and bon mots:
Nothing, done well, is still nothing.
It was always Father
who got to decide what is something
and what is not.

Sometimes I lie awake beside my husband
and feel them both there,
conversing again,
the way they did before the divorce.
That smart, sometimes sad, talk
before there was no talk between them at all,
just lawyers and grandmothers
taking their brittle sides,
hurling those insults
and waiting to see who got the kids.

Sometimes I lie beside my husband at night
and don't feel them at all,
and then I am a very small and empty person,
maybe too small to make any difference in this world.
There's a wave of loss,
drowning me in my bed.

But when I wake up and look in the mirror
I hear my mother say,
Get your hair out of your eyes;
you have the most beautiful face I've ever seen.
And I remember my father's hand
sweeping my bangs to the side.
I get a cup of coffee and dress for work,
wearing Mother's watch
and the gold Star of David,
Father gave me when I turned sixteen.

November Song

The fierce winter wind
has blown all the leaves
off the trees, leaving them bald
like the very sick,
or like men and women
inclining toward old age.

The bare trees
still house bird and squirrel nests
clumped among the branches.
This is what she sees bundled up
on the front porch in her old armchair,
feet warmed atop a large white dog,
Persian cat on her lap.

What she smells is wood smoke,
her peach pies cooling
on the kitchen windowsill.
She feels the nip of chilly air
against her cheeks.

What she hears is the dog's soft snore,
the purr of the cat settled beneath her hand,
from a distance, a chain saw,
and, closer, the tinny strains of music
from her neighbor's TV.

She is thinking about
all her old lovers,
tries to count them,
tries to remember their names,
or even just their faces,
where they fit into her life.
Some are gone now.
Some, like the trees,
have lost their hair;
some have grown a paunch,
pick their careful way along her sidewalk.

Some remember to call her
every year on her birthday
and that is like a thousand sparklers
fizzing silver and gold
against the black, black velvet of the night.

Lilacs
(for TR)

I'm not sure how long it'll take,
but it won't be pretty,
and I don't need your help doing it.
Do not feel
you have to wait around
and watch me die.
There is no need to cling.

If you fall in love with another man
and hop on that train,
I'll wave to you from the station.
I'll watch your face
pressed up against the window,
your features a blur
of distance and speed.

I'll go home and make a margarita,
light a joint,
slide into my hammock,
dream of oysters on the BBQ,
line-dancing music,
and all my beautiful lovers.
I will dream of the past.

And, if, when I awake
in late afternoon sun,
I see your grey eyes, curious, staring,
I will take your hand,
and together we can breathe in
the lilacs growing over the fence.
The pale-purple kind,
so improbably fragrant
though the blossoms last
only a few brief weeks
in spring.

GRIEF'S WEIRD SISTER

Your whole body aches,
although no specific part really hurts.
I understand.
I have been such a body.
I have cried for a year,
a box of Kleenex
on the passenger seat of my car.

I could say to you, time.
I could say to you
rice pudding cold from the fridge
or the smell of bread baking
in your neighbor's oven.

I could say an aquamarine sea,
the surface broken by spinner dolphins.
I could say a field of yellow jonquils—
the one behind your best friend's house.
I could say, stroke the hot fur of your black dog
after he has been lying in the grass.

He would sit at your feet
if you stretched in the porch swing
on a summer night.
The navy-blue sky.
A gibbous moon. Mysterious stars,
one briefly streaking across the heavens,
trailing its tail of silver and white.

You tell me
you remember the blue chair opening its arms
and your husband settling in.
The familiar rattle of the Sunday paper.
The dark, rich smell of his coffee.
The light slanting across your Turkish carpet
and the orange cat in his lap.

When you get into the chair
your cat just looks at you
from across the room,
accusation in her eyes.
You rattle the paper but
it doesn't sound right.
You drink coffee which has gone tepid
while you think about anything else.

Once, I sat in that chair,
stared at the walls
and at the floor while my coffee
lost its heat.
I stayed that way for months,
the gate locked,
the shades drawn,
the phone unplugged.
I was trying to figure it out
in the dark.
Even when my cat finally relented
and lay in my lap,
I barely noticed
her presence.

So now,
I say to you, time.
I say cold rice pudding.
The black dog,
and the sweet sound of his tail
thump, thump, thumping
in your entry hall.

You say to me,
I am not hungry.
I say, you don't have to be hungry
to enjoy rice pudding.
You say to me it is raining.
I say to you, take an umbrella,
walk down to the water's edge.
Unclip the leash;
let the dog play
in the wet sand.
Lean against the lime-green bench
and watch the sailboats skim in and out
of the stippled bay.

A Gift

Sometimes I remember to love how the moon organizes the oceans. Sometimes I forget to love. Sometimes I am so caught up being the wheel, whipped around by life, I forget to be the still center. Sometimes I remember her life—how kaleidoscopic it was, how quietly imperfect. Sometimes I remember her long illness, her death. I wear her watch and feel her pulse beating in my wrist.

My life, too, has been composed of tessellated bits: meals, trips, jobs, books, men I have followed like a gypsy, or one of those wind-up toys which hits a wall and careens off in another direction. Once, lying on the couch, my head on her lap as she brushed my hair, I heard her tell a friend, *Sometimes I think this is not my daughter; she is so dark and beautiful, so bright and so brash, the gypsies must have left her on our doorstep.* Sometimes I forget that she is gone.

I scuff along the beach for hours. Sometimes I hear a voice, a laugh. I look to my right and am surprised not to find her there. The wind blows black curls into my eyes which tear up. I walk around a small harbor, sand gritty between my toes, and halyards ring against sailboat masts. I see waves of wild foam, fragments of smoke-colored clouds against the sky, a bewildering blue. In passing, a woman, a stranger, hands me an unbroken shell. It is conical, silver and rose—the colors of dawn. Overhead, a hungry osprey on the wing. Wriggling in her talons, a fish. She will tear it to pieces for her nestlings.

INTO NIGHT

I.
Just before dusk, the dog and I
stroll past high-rise buildings,
white-table-cloth restaurants
where early evening diners sit outside
despite the noise from drivers
crawling through rush-hour traffic
and honking their horns.

At one table,
women sip white wine,
talk about their husbands,
whisper about their lovers.
The dog ignores them all, sniffs his way along.
Overhead, pigeons preen in the lingering light.

II.
We cross railroad tracks
into a nearby town.
Stores, the shoe repair, the bakery, are all closing.
Yellow lights from above
soften the sidewalk, reflect on cars
parked along the roadway.

We pass an inn,
old people on porch swings.
From inside, Frank Sinatra croons,
Make it one for my baby,
and one more for the road.
A woman sings out, *Your dog's beautiful,*
and I wave and smile.
He's not really my dog, I reply.
What we say is not always what is true.

III.
We walk into a village, thatched-roof
cottages and small shops around a village green.
The dog races through the grass,
comes back with wet feet and a wagging tail.
From the pub's open door,
a white rectangle of light,
rowdy laughter and the click click
of balls on a pool table.
Two men in tee-shirts,
though the evening is turning cool,
mumble, *See ya tomorrow*,
climb into their dusty pick-ups
and drive away.

Cottage windows shimmer with blue light
and we can just hear bits
of game shows, talent contests and family dramas.
Chimneys puff smoke.

When the glow of the village dims,
the dog slows, begins to whimper
as if we were leaving behind
all that comforts us.

IV.
At the edge of the woods,
I hear no sound of women or men.
No one weeps for a lost love
or confesses feeling guilty,
or burns with shame.
No one speaks my name.

I search for a path, call to the dog
and find he has vanished.

Behind me, instead,
snuffling and a pair of amber eyes.
In the dog's place, a gray wolf.
I say, *The dog is missing.*
The wolf says, *Never mind.*

Deep night has arrived.
The wolf keeps a steady pace,
navigates through the trees;
I follow as well as I can
although the brambles seem to part for him,
and close up around me.
Bats flutter through branches;
an owl hoots to claim territory.

I am tired.
I grab the wolf's tail
and lie on his back, clutch
the coarse fur so I won't fall off.
I am closer to the ground now,
closer to the rustling
of the tiny creatures in the underbrush.
The forest is alive.
I can hear it breathe.

BRIDGE

I imagine that
my mother, father and stepfather
find a fourth for bridge,
the newly deceased widow of a navy admiral.
They set up a card table and chairs
between the gravestones.
Visitors with their flowers walk right by,
looking down at the earth,
pausing to read the markers.

I can see the cards and
a bowl of Licorice Allsorts.
My father liked to eat that candy
with those layers of black, white
and peppermint green.
And bone china cups of tea
which the women sip
after taking their tricks.

Creeping into the scene,
a fluffy-tailed red fox,
one shy coyote,
and even a small herd of deer
stepping out from under the trees,
and coming to lie in the sun
at my mother's feet.

Sitting on a hill
half-hidden by wood ferns,
I am still,
waiting for my turn.

ACKNOWLEDGEMENTS

"A Gift." *Mudfish*, vol # 18 (2013)

"Barking, Pt. Reyes."
  Sow's Ear Competition finalist (2010)
  Nimrod Literary Award, Pablo Neruda Prize 1st Place (2012)
  Northern Colorado Writers Poetry Contest 1st Place (2013)
  New Millennium Awards 1st Place (2014)
  Mudfish Poetry Prize and nominated for a Pushcart Prize (2017)

"Because." *Worcester Review*, nominated for a Pushcart Prize (2011)

"Black Lizard." *Hunger Mountain* # 18 (2012)
  Nimrod Literary Award Pablo Neruda Prize finalist (2012)
  Paumanok Poetry Award (2013)
  Lothlorien Poetry Journal (2021)
  Lothlorien Poetry Journal Anthology (2021)

"Brass Key." *California Quarterly* (2014)

"Bridge." *Silver Birch Press* online (2021)

"Cakes." *Marin Poetry Center Anthology* (2005)
  Good News (2007)

"Dear Father." Paumanok Poetry Award (2012)
  Nimrod (2012)

"Dolphins in Shark Bay…" Award of Merit in League of Minnesota Poets Contest (2009)
  Canary (2019)

"Dropping Acid…" Sow's Ear Poetry Competition finalist (2011)
  Atlanta Review International Poetry Competition Prize (2013)
  The Ledge Poetry Prize 3rd place (2013)
  Poetry and Places online (2020)

"Drug Wars…" *Adroit Journal* (2011)

"Exotic Feline Rescue…" Sow's Ear Poetry Competition, finalist (2010)

"Grandfather's Funeral." Nimrod Poetry Prize Pablo Neruda Award semi-finalist (2010)
Chapter and Verse Anthology (2010)

"Hit and Run." *Wisconsin Review* (2002)
Poetalk (2004)
Rain Tiger (2005)

"Grief's Weird Sister." Mudfish Poetry Prize finalist, published in *Mudfish* # 23 (2021)

"I Keep an Apartment…" *Nimrod*, Atlanta Review International Merit Award

"Iceland, Summer." *Poetry and Places* online (2020)

"Ida's Wine." *Adroit Journal* (2011)

"Impact." *Marin Poetry Center Anthology* (2002)

"Improvisation…" *Barnwood* online (2004)
Good News (2005)

"In a Berlin Bar." Paumanok Poetry Award 1st Place (2012)
Nimrod Literary Award finalist (2012)
Slippery Elm (2013)

"Kobe, Japan." League of Minnesota Poets Contest 1st place (2006)
Pride in Poetry finalist; published in anthology (2009)
Marin Poetry Center Anthology (2007)
Good News (2009)
Poetry and Places online (2021)

"Lilacs," *Marin Poetry Center Anthology* (2007)
Maggie Meyer Contest 1st place (2012)
Nimrod's Pablo Neruda Prize finalist, *Nimrod* (2012)
Jewish Women's Literary Annual (2014)

"Listening to Sam…" Lunarosity online (2006)

"Lost Art." (as "Light as a Particle, as a Wave") Ina Coolbrith Grand Prize (2008)

"Luna." (as "Past Luna") Nimrod Literary Award finalist *Nimrod* (2012)

"Noon." Ina Coolbrith Contest 1st place (2011)

Jewish Women's Literary Annual (2012)

"Olive Oil." Allen Ginsberg Award 1st place (2010)

    Chapter and Verse Anthology (2010)

    Enizagam (2012)

    Mudfish Poetry Prize finalist (2017)

    Poetry and Places online (2021)

    Lothlorien Poetry Journal (2021)

    Lothlorien Poetry Journal Anthology (2021)

"On Spending Just…" *Caveat Lector* (2009)

    Chapter and Verse Anthology (2010)

"Roses and Moons." *California Quarterly* (2014)

"Shut the Door." Frances Locke Memorial Poetry Award finalist (2001)

    River Styx Poetry Contest finalist (2001)

    Lothlorien Poetry Journal online (2022)

"Sika Deer." League of Minnesota Poets Contest 1st place (2009)

    Oberon (2010)

    Chapter and Verse Anthology (2010)

"Standing Dead." Dana Awards pre-finalist (2003)

"Sunset." (as "Bats at Sunset") *Jewish Women's Literary Annual* (2012)

"Swimming Lesson." League of Minnesota Poets, Jeanette Hinds Memorial Grand Prize Award, Citation (2009)

    *Caveat Lector (*2009)

"The Baby." *Peralta Art and Literary Journal* (2000);

    Marin Poetry Center Anthology (2003)

    Sky Blue Waters Contest 2nd place (2003)

    Good News (2004)

    Rain Tiger Heart of the Poet feature online (2005)

    Grandmother Earth Poetry Award 1st place (2010)

"The Matah on Kibbutz…" *Jewish Women's Literary Annual* (2005)

"The Road." *Jewish Women's Literary Annual* (2015)

    Mudfish (2017)

    Lothlorien Poetry Journal online (2021)

Lothlorien Poetry Journal Anthology (2021)

"Two Jews, Truck Stop…" Atlanta Review International Poetry
Competition Merit Award (2012)

Nimrod Literary Awards Pablo Neruda Prize finalist (2012)

Poetry and Places (2020)

Lothlorien Poetry Journal online (2021)

Lothlorien Poetry Journal Anthology (2021)

"Underpants." *Iconoclast* (2007)

A Women's Writing Salon online (2022)

"Water and Salt." *Marin Poetry Center Anthology* (2010)

"Winter, Lower Longley…" Gemini Magazine Poetry Open
2nd place, published online May (2018)

Poetry and Places online (2020)